T0113677

RIO ABAJO RIO
river beneath river

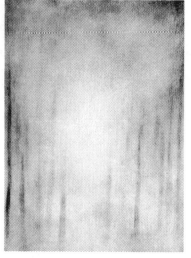

BARBARA GRENFELL FAIRHEAD

RIO ABAJO RIO

RIO ABAJO RIO

RIVER BENEATH RIVER

Barbara Grenfell Fairhead

Publication © Modjaji Books 2021
Text © Barbara Grenfell Fairhead 2021
First published in 2021 by Hands-On Books
www.modjajibooks.co.za

ISBN 978-1-928433-32-3

Cover artist: Trilby Krepelka
Book design and layout: Liz Gowans

Set in Myriad Pro Light

for

JACQUES and JAN

with love and gratitude

IN THE MIDDLE OF THE STORY OF MY LIFE
I AWOKE IN A DARK WOOD,
WHERE THE TRUE WAY WAS WHOLLY LOST

Dante Alighieri

WIND-COME-OUT-OF-NO-WHERE

Wind—come-out-of-No-Where—
one Hear tell of it—
a Whisper—
a Word—
by one who claim—Know—

turn away—
not Wind-from-No-Where—

from one—who Know—
Listen—
Hear—

No-Thing—

*

Wind—not-come-from-Any-Where—
Sudden it come—
it come—like Haunt—
a dark Wind—
whereof one keep silent—

a Sudden rush of Wind—
dark Wind—come-out-of-No-Where—

dark Shadow on dark Water—
and River—
what She Say—

River Say—

No-Thing—

*

WOMAN – SHE-WOLF

She-Wolf—close by—
Woman—Feel Her—

Woman Touch Place between both Eye—
Mark-of-Blood-Pattern—

put Hand here—
She Touch Throat—it Speak   not Words—

put Hand here—
She Touch Heart—She Feel She-Wolf—in Heart—

Woman Say—
this Loba—bring such Alone in Heart—
this—She-Wolf-with-Limp—
full-grown—Female—not young—
Story—not tell—

Loba—on path—same like Wolf-Woman—
Story—not tell—

cast out Pack—perhaps—
Wolf-Pack—Life—Hard—Fierce—

Wolf-Woman—Life—same—
this Woman—never Belong—
any-where—
never want it—
Deep in Heart—

and now—this She-Wolf—with No-Name—
why She come this Place—
maybe share—same Strong—Feel in Heart—
like Wolf-Woman—
share same—Sad—
walk alone—in Forest—
Listen River—

how—Call—come—to—Wolf-Woman—

it come—
like—Deep Pain—
more Deep—like Mountain—
more Deep—like Black Night—
more Deep—like Great Mist—

like—Listen—Howl—
like—no—Ear—Hear—Tears—
like Blood-Call—Wild-Empty—

like—Big Pain in Heart—
Sad—
like—dark Haunt Wind—

*

where She Know it—
it come from—She-Wolf-Pattern—
from—Scent-of-Foot-Print—
from—Ancient-Memories—
Long-Before-Count—

Woman—Know—Loba—here—now—

She—wait—
She—watch—

*

SANGRE

She first Hear Call—Day She Find Sangre—
Hear—long—Howl—in torrent of Leaf—
some Leaf—Stain—Bright-Red Blood—
some Blood—begin go Black—

Hear Call—from Wide-Open-Eye—
from—Strong-Dead-Face—

She Child then—

*

and what Say of Her—

She—also Name—
Hembra de Lobos—
Wolf-Woman—

Stranger ask—
why—Wolf-Woman here—
People—not see Wolf—

Wolf stay—Woman stay—

not—See—Wolf—

no—

*

when She Child—She think—all People Live—same—

She smile—
Sangre Show Her—other Story—

Sangre—
where He go—

*

Wind blow through Trees—
Fall-Time—all Leaf look—not same—
way Song—not same—

Big-Shine make Leaf—not look same—
Warm-Leaf—
First-Blood Leaf—
Mix-Sky Leaf—
fall down on Her—

what they Say—

She See Small-Wolf behind Eye—
She Feel Hackle rise on Back-of-Neck—
Sangre—

no—
Sangre—He not here—

maybe—other time—
maybe—other Life—
maybe—same—other—Story—
maybe—Child—Hide—in—Woman—

*

Woman sit—gaze Water—
dark Water—
Woman Listen River—
River Voice—dark like Water—
no Light in Voice—no Light in dark River—
Dios de los Rios—
why Voice—always other—always same—
why take all River-Story away—
how then—
Woman Listen River—

River not Speak like Wind—
Wind-come-from-No-Where—come like strange—
like Haunt—
like—Face Big-Round—Live behind Mountain—
Big-Round—not warm like Big-Shine—
Big-Round—Hang in Night-Sky—
Big-Round—
so still—
so bright—
so silent—

dark River—say No-Thing—

*

HOMBRE

Hombre wear—Animal Skin on both Hand—
soft Animal Skin—like Hand-Shoe—

Hombre make Hand-Shoe—soft Skin—Young-Wolf-Cub—
keep both Hand warm—
Hombre set Trap—close by—Two-Rocks—

Gather—arm-full Leaf—
throw Leaf—High—in Air—
watch Leaf—fly like small Bird—
begin slow fall—
beautiful—Bright-Blood Leaf—
also Leaf—same like Big-Shine—
some dark—
like—
Dry-Blood—

He watch—
Leaf—
drift—
slow—
slow—
down—
cover—
Tree-Branch-and-Noose Trap—

Hombre walk on—

Child wait—Big-Fright—inside Body—

Child Heart—beat fast—in Throat—Heart Say—

Bad Thing—come happen—

She—Feel—Earth—open—

Feel—
Dark Power—
climb up—
from Deep Place—
climb up—
through Feet—
fill whole Body—

Angry—
Black—
Rage—

Angry—
like Dark-Cloud—make Earth-Shake—

Hombre—Listen—rustle sound—Bright-Blood Leaf—
Big-Shine grow hot—many Leaf—fall—
and Wind—
Wind-come-out-of-No-Where—
give Tree-Branch—rattle-sound—like old Bones—

Child follow—
soft-soft—like Fox—
may-be—no sound—

like Wild-Cat—move—Tree—other Tree—

*

Tree-Branch-Spring—pull Leg High—
Wind carry—Long-Pain-Howl—
thong bite—Blood-Flesh—
Noose cut into Flesh—like Teeth—
She-Wolf Hang—Leg High—Leg Break—
Wind full—Scream—Blood-Flesh—
Blood-Pain—
White—Teeth—Gnaw—Leg Bone—

get free—
get free—

*

Child stand—
Head rest on tall Tree—
Hand over Mouth—Shake—
Hand hush Sobs—
Sobs—well up in Throat—
well up—
like Dark Water—
like Swollen River after Storm—
like Dark Wind Rage through—Bright-Blood Leaf—

like Pain—run through Body—throb in Throat—
like raw Howl—
Long—Slow—Death—
Pain—

Fear not get free—

Fear not get free—

Sudden—Child See—
Hombre—Stand—with Back to Her—
Stand—so still—

He Look—down—See Dark Form—
He Stare—down—See Dead Body—
Eye—open—

how Dead Face look—so Alive—

Child move back—
not make sound—
Child full Pain—
full Fear—

Wind come—

Wind-not-come-from-Any-Where—
Sudden—
it come—Sudden—like Storm—
Hombre Look round Him—

Sudden—
Hombre afraid—

many Leaf rise up in Wind—
Red Leaf—Bright—like Fresh-Blood—
blow against Him—
blow Hard—
Hard-Wind—Fresh-Blood Leaf—make Fear—
like not-Know-Thing—come make Sickness—
Black Fear—and Blood-Shadow—
all He See—Blood—
Fresh-Blood—
Hombre pull hat—cover Face—

*

behind Tree—
Child Hide—See Small Creature—
make Panic—
run—
Hide—in thick bush—

No-Thing move—
Silence—more Fright than Wind—

Hombre push hat back—
light pipe—

Hombre wait—
wait for—

wait for—

Hombre—Sudden—full—Not-Know—

He Look—all-over—
See No-Thing—
He finish pipe—

Hombre bend down—
See Blood—
Blood on Face of She-Wolf—
Fresh-Blood on white Teeth—
Pain-Snarl—on Face of Dead She-Wolf—
See dark Dry-Blood on Boot—
See Fresh Bright-Blood—on Boot—

Hombre cut tight thong—
See—Blood—on—Hand-Shoe—

Hombre—throw—Leg-with-Break—
on—ground—
take Noose—
put Noose in Bag—

Dead—She-Wolf—
Leg-with-Break—
Place—where She gnaw—get free—
Big Blood Pool in Forest—

Blood—begin—look—Black—
Hombre—make—Bad—Thing—
Hombre—take—Life—She-Wolf—

all place Hombre Look—See—Blood—
Eye—See—Blood—
Fear—See—Blood—

*

Child wait—watch Hombre go—
Child make—Power-Day-Dream—
Hombre—Long-Way-Away—

Child go Look in bush—

*

She name Him Sangre—
for Blood on coat—

*

LOBA

two yellow Eye—Sharp Eye—not blink—
all Wolf Know—when Loba stand at Source—
She Stare down—all Female-Wolf rival—

no equal in Pack—for She-Wolf like Loba—
She—drink—first—at—Source—
Sweet-Water—

only First Wolf—ever drink—Source—
ever drink—Sweet-Water—
Source-Water—same—not same—like River—
Source-Water—always Clear—

no Male—no Female—ever—breed—
Blood-Mountain-Pack—
if not—See—Face—in Still Water—
Water-of-Source—

LISTEN CALL

Wolf-Woman sit on River bank—
Listen far-away Call—
Listen Wolf-Howl—
far-away—

Feet in River—
Listen—
never-same—always-same—River-Flow—

Woman—Listen—long—long—Howl—
Woman—Listen—Howl—Deep—in—Bones—
Wolf-Woman—Feel—Howl—come—
from—
Woman-Body—

Wind-from-No-Where—come carry Woman-Howl—
all way River—
all way up River—
all way down River—

Sudden—
Howl—make—change—in—Woman—
Wind Touch Body—like Pair Hand—
Strong—Hand—like—gentle—
blow—through—Body—

Shape—New—Body—

Shape—Feet-with-Claw—
Shape—Prick-Ear—Wolf-Ear—
Shape—Wolf-Body—
Strong Skull—
Neck—reach—down—long—Wolf-Spine—
long Wolf-Tail—

Wind come—
Wind-come-from-No-Where—
Wind-from-No-Where—bring—Memory—
bring Ancient-Wolf-Soul—

bring every Hair—
every Whisker—
each In-Breath—
each Out-Breath—

make Blood Alive—
make Breath Alive—

Wind—come-from-No-Where—
Breathe Deep into Wolf—

*

SOURCE

Loba Know dark Wind Speak Soon—
can Feel Pack—far-away—

Loba—
old She-Wolf now—

gaze Still Water—Deep Source-Water—
Deep as Mountain—
See Eye—like same—Young-Eye—
clear in Water—
Loba—Look—Deep—into—Eye—

She—not—afraid—
Eye—not—afraid—

Wind-come-from-No-Where—
blow over Mountain—Big-Round go-sleep behind—

blow over Wide-Place where Sad-Grass Sing—
blow through all Forest Tree—

Wind blow Soft—
Wind blow—Small Wave on Source-Water—
Loba-Face—Break All-Over—
Face—Eye—Ear—
go—other—Place—

maybe go Wind—

*

Loba—See—Break in Face—
other Wolf-Eye—Know—
Pack—Know—
not need for Tell—

Blood-Know Beyond All Thing—

Night—
Wind come—
Dark—Night—Wind—
Dark—Night—carry—Howl—

Wind—blow—Wild—only—She—Feel—
Feel—Tear-Apart—
how She not Know—

She See it once—in other—
not—need—second—visit—

Loba See Big-Round in Night-Sky—
what She do—

Some Hear Stay—Some Hear Go—
She—Know—She Go—

yet—leave—make Sad—
make—Heavy—in—Heart—
make—Full-of-Want—She—young—again—
like—New-Female—

other She-Wolf come this Day—
come to Source—
this Last-Day—First-Day—

New-Female—first time at Source—
so quick—
She—make—last—leap—to—Source—

like Bird—
how—long—and—light—She—look—
how—Strong—

*

Loba—like—that—once—

all—Males—Look—Loba—
quick-quick—
Look-away—
She—Loba—First-Female—

Look away—
Look away—

Blood-Word-of-Pack—happen—
Swift—
Clean—

all young Male-Wolf Know—
Live-Strong demand this—

*

BONE-DREAM

Dream Bones Call—Hembra de Lobos—
other Name—Wolf-Woman—
Bones Call on Dream-Wind—
they Say—
Come—Gather—Bones—
Wolf-Spirit not rest—
all Bones not Make-Pattern—

*

Hembra de Lobos Dream—
See—Young-Child—follow—Hombre—
Child See Dead She-Wolf—
See Not-Broken Dead Face—
Wolf-Eye—wide-open—
All Light gone—

Hombre—take—only—Wolf-Pelt—
leave Wolf-Body—

Hombre—not—Know—Bone-Song—
not Know—Bones—Listen—Song—

Call come to Woman—Sad Dark Dream—

Sound like—Wind Sad also—
Woman Hear Call—even-She-Sleep—
Feel—Heart Break—even-She-Sleep—
Dark Forest Wind carry Call—
Hembra de Lobos—
Wolf-Woman—have Sad Dream—
must tell Wind—

Woman sit up—
Sudden—
Awake—

Hear Young-Child Sob—

must go—
must go—
now—

*

Big-Round—Face-of-Blood—
Rise over Forest—
Big-Ache-Dark—
of Forest—

Big-Round—Hang in Night-Sky—
Face Blood-Stain—

full of Long-For—

Big-Round have Blood-Face—
Ghost—of—Blood—Silence—

long—Dark—Night—of—Blood-Pain—
long—Dark—Night—of—Blood-Shame—

Wolf-Woman Know—This go in Memories—
No-Thing ever Forget—in Memories—
not Blood-Shame—

Big-Round—Send Fresh-Blood-Light—
Find Bones—Find Big Rock—
Find Tree—
watch-over—
Child Tears—

*

Wolf-Woman Stand—
five Steps—close—Place-make-Blood-Pain—
close—Shame-Place—
Place—tight—Noose—cut—Flesh—
cut Deep—close—Bone—
Noose—choke Blood—
Flesh—Break—open—

Leg Bone—
Break—

Wolf-Woman Listen—Tooth-Gnaw Sound—
Sharp Teeth make on Leg—

Listen—
Big-Blood-Pain-Howl—

not—end—

not—end—

not—end—

*

Young-Child—Many-Sob—

Hear—Wolf-Howl on Dark Wind—
loud—
more loud—
Black—Blood—Pain—
Blood—make—Black Blood Pool—

Woman—Listen—Raw—Howl—

Listen—Die—Howl—
Blood—Howl—
Slow—
Loba—
Head—
fall—

Blood—on Wolf-Body—

Life—
gone—

Loba—

*

DREAM BONE SONG

Big-Round—Weep Blood-Tears—over Bones—
Blood-Stain—on White Bone—
Blood-Stain—on Wolf-Skull—

Wolf-Woman Kneel on Forest Leaf—

Feel Child Pain—

Feel Child Tears—
Feel—Big Pain in Heart—

Wolf-Woman feel Touch—fall Leaf—
all colour—Leaf fall—on Her—
like Tears in Wind—

like Wind-come-from-No-Where—
Sudden it come—
it come—like Sad—like Haunt—
it Say—
close Eye—See Child-Face—
Feel Small Child-Body—how it Shake—
Feel Woman-Body—how it Shake—

Woman take off—Dress—
make Hair loose—
pick up Bag-for-Gather-Bones—
pick up Cloth Rags—
prepare for Clean Bones—

Woman begin rock—
Slow—
way Mother rock Child—

Words for Gather-Bones—
begin Sing—through Her—

Song—Sound like River—
like cool Water—on hot Day—
like Wind-come-from-No-Where—
Breathe—Soft—Soft—

Look—

Bones—
begin—
move—

Slow—

Slow—

Bones—Make—Pattern—

*

Wind—
Wild-as-Storm-Wind—
Wind carry White Face of Spirit Wolf—
Make-Fly over Bones—
like Shine—
like flood of Silence—
like Breath—
begin—Fly—

and Howl—

long Howl—till every Bone—Make-Pattern—

all Body Bones—
all Long Leg Bones—
all Thin Breath Bones—
all down—Bone-Curve-of-Wolf-Back—
all small Bones Make-Pattern—
all way—to—end—Wolf-Tail—

Wind—Breathe—Slow—Over—Wolf-Skull—
all—Forest—Still—

*

Song—finish—
Forest Breathe again—

*

Hembra de Lobos Spread Cloth Rags—
for Wrap Bones—
Touch Blood-Mark—
All Body Speak Old-Power Words—

Hembra de Lobos—
take Leg Bone with Blood-Break—
Weep for Blood-Break—
Weep for long Night—Blood-Pain—
Weep for Bright-Blood Spill—
Weep for Dark Night—
Weep for Small Pup—
alone—

Woman Shed many Tear—
wash away—dark Blood-Stain—
off Break Leg Bone—
wash away—
Death—Hombre make—to Flesh—to Blood—
to She-Wolf—
who come—out of No-Time—
come out of Mist-of-Great-No-Thing—
Long-Before-Count—

She Sing—Soft—
Wrap Break-Leg in white cotton Cloth—
place Leg close to Heart—
close—
to Mother-Breast—
close to—
Safest-Place-in-World—

*

RIVER

Old She-Wolf-with-Limp—
watch Woman—
from Hide in thick River-Willow—
watch—
want—
long for—
as only Wolf Know—

*

Wolf-Woman—Hembra de Lobos—
People call Her—Wolf-Woman—
She born—Deep Know of Other—

She Know—after Gather-Bones—
Time of Clean—

She—pull—Dress—over—Head—
Stand—Naked—
Naked—like—White Bone—
Listen—River-Song—

Wolf-Woman enter lazy River—

Slow as Dream—
Slow as Forget—
She close Eye—

Body float with Stream—
Feel Soft River Touch—all Naked Bone of Body—
begin Sing—Naked-Bone-Song—
Hair—float—free—in—Water—

She—Feel—River—Pull—
Deep dark quiet of—not-See—not-Know—
River-Mystery—

how She ache for it—
Old-River-Mystery—
Old—Before—Count—

River-Water move Slow—
River get Shine—
See all of Sky—in Water—
See Big-Round Rise—Hang in Night-River—
See Fire-Sparks—All-Many—Night-Sky—
all Shine in River—

Wolf-Woman—Call—to Darkness—

Call to Deep—Dark—quiet—not-See—River-Mystery—

Wolf-Woman—reach—out—open Arm—
ask—River-Mystery—
enter—Deep place in Heart—
She—feel—Smooth—River-Bed—
Soft—Sand—
She—sit—River-Bed—
watch—Hand—full—Sand—
drift—away—in—River-Stream—

Wolf-Woman—long—drift—away—
in—cool—Stream—
long—for—River—carry—Her—
all—way—Great Water—

Wolf-Woman—Eye shut—Many-Ear—not Hear—
She give Her Body—Her Song—
All of Her—
to River—

to always-same—
never-same—
River-Journey—

River Say—

No-Thing—

Wolf-Woman—Call to River—
one last time—

River-Mystery not answer—

Wolf-Woman Listen—
Many-Ear—
She Hear No-Thing—

Wolf-Woman Feel—
Breath-Cage—
Soon burst—

Call come—from Forest—
Come back—Forest Say—

Wolf-Woman-Body—Call to Her—

need Breathe—
need Breathe—

Wind-from-No-Where—
Wind—First-of-Things—
Wind—Last-of-Things—

Wind-come-out-of-No-Where—
come—like Small Swift Bird—
come—bring—
Soft Song of Ancestor-Know—
come—
bring Heart-Memory—

Wind-from-No-Where—
Breathe—
Wolf-Woman—out—River—

*

Wind-from-No-Where—
Angry—
Angry—like—Storm—
Wind—make Big Rage in River-Water—
like Waves—

Wind-from-No-Where—See Woman—
Soon—
very close—
Lose All Thing—

Wind See Wolf-Woman—
come close—Fall into Sleep—

Some People not Wake—Such Sleep—
River take them all way—Great Water—

See Hembra de Lobos—
come close—Edge-of-World—
not good place—go Sleep—

can lose—Most Precious Gift—
not come back—

Woman Know—
She come back—One Time—

not get help—
Wind-come-out-of-No-Where—
Two time—

Wolf-Woman—go sit on rock—
Listen River—
Deep-Listen all Heart Say—

Heart Say—Woman go wrong way in River—
Woman—go—end—River—Great Water—
Woman—not Find—what She Look for—

Woman—want—Know—What—Make—Her—

Woman—need Find—Where—She—Begin—

not Look River—
River keep Mystery—
Woman Listen River—
River already not there—

Wolf-Woman—Feel Shame—
Woman—watch—All—Hembra de Lobos—do—
She Say—
not Look—All Eye—Woman throw away Gift—

Woman—full of tired—
fall asleep—

*

NIGHT-SPARK

Night-Spark—close—Big-Round—
make Light—So Bright—
Wake Wind—
Wind—come-out-of-No-Where—
Wind Awake—Fierce Wind—
not-come-from-Any-Where—

Fierce-Wind—come-from-No-Where—
race through Forest—
race through Forest Trees—
Shake Forest Trees—not—one—Leaf—left on Branch—
Fierce-Wind—bend naked Trees—low on ground—
blow—Forest Leaf—High above Trees—
High into Night-Sky—

no Leaf left in Forest—

*

Wolf-Woman Wake—See Leaf—fly away—
Night-Spark make Leaf—fly in Night-Sky—

She-Wolf Wake—She See Leaf fly away—
She-Wolf Stay in River-Willow-Hide—

Storm-Wind—blow Leaf—
High as Night-Spark—

Woman See—Fire—
Flash—Flash—Flash—
High in Night-Sky—

See Fire-Snake—
cross—Dark-Light-Dark Sky—

See many Fire-Snake race cross Dark Sky—

Listen Big-Voice-Roar—Shake Forest—
Shake She-Wolf in River-Willow-Hide—

Big-Noise-in-Sky—make Forest-Floor Shake Hard—
Wolf-Woman Hold tight on Tree—
watch all Leaf burn in Night-Sky—
See Fire-Flash-in-Sky—make like Day—
Wolf-Woman—See all thing—
See all World—like Day—
Sudden—
Dark again—

all grow Still—
Wind grow quiet—
Night-Spark grow Small—

Night-Spark—fly away—
Hide behind Dark Sky—

not Leaf in Sky—
not Leaf—Forest-Floor—
Earth Dark Place—

Woman leave Tree—

Look far out over Forest—

*

BONES

Wind—come-from-No-Where—Call—Wolf-Woman—
blow Soft in Face Wolf-Woman—
Change-Wind—Wind-of-Other—
open Many-Eye in Face Wolf-Woman—
Soft Wind blow down Throat—
Wake Breath for Sing—
Wolf-Woman—open Heart—

Bones Know—
how Wind make Soft change—

Wind bring Woman—other Name—
Wolf-Woman close Eye—Listen Name—
Listen—

La Huesera—

Bone-Woman—

*

Wind-from-No-Where—Say—
many other Bones—La Huesera must Find—

She—Find—Bones—close—River—
now must Look—Forest—
all Forest—many Bones—
come Make-Pattern—

Bone-Woman Stand Still—
Look Forest—
what She See—
Woman See—Bones—many Bones—
La Huesera—See Bones—all place She Look—
White Bones—
Naked White Bones—

*

All Day—She-Wolf-with-Limp follow Her—
Wolf-Woman not See—

She-Wolf Hide in bush—
Hide behind Tree—
She-Wolf track good—
She follow Scent-Path—

She-Wolf Hide—Deep in rocks—

Woman Smell Blue-Flowers—
Blue-Flowers make Smell-of-Smoke—
make Blue-Memory—

Blue-Flowers grow—in Blood-Rich Forest-Soil—
not—Forget—Mother-of-Sangre—
not—Forget—Blood-of-She-Wolf kill in Trap—
Smoke-Smell-of-Blue-Flowers—not Forget—
She-Wolf Bones—also buried—
close Blue-Forest-Flowers—

*

All Day Bone-Woman walk Forest—
Gather-Bones—
Heavy Bones—
Wolf Bones—
Rabbit Bones—Large-Hare Bones—
Owl—Crow—Fox Bones—
Deer Bones—
Raven Bones—

Bone-Woman Gather Small Bones—
Creature Live River-Bank—
Beaver Bones—

Otter Bones—
Water Rat Bones—

Bone-Woman—carry Bones—
leave close Two-Rocks—
same Place—She-Wolf—caught-in-Trap—
Place all Bones Sleep—

same Place Sangre Find—Hide-Place—
same Place—Hombre—Fear—go—
Place Earth Hold—She-Wolf-Blood—

Heart-Speak-Place—of Blue-Forest-Flowers—

Bone-Woman bring last Bones—

All Day—Bone-Woman—Sing over Bones—
Scratch Small Pattern—in Forest-Sand—
Sing—till Bones Make-Pattern—

Wolf-Body—
Feel again—Strong Legs—run—
long Spine—
Strong Skull—

Woman Say—all Bones—Find-Pattern—

in Bone-Woman Song—

Raven—Owl—Crow—
Feel Strong Body—Foot-Claws—
Seize prey—

Small Bones from Rat—
Heavy Bones from Deer—
all Find-Pattern—Full-Heart-Speak—in Bone-Woman Song—

Bone-Woman make Bone-Sleep-Place—
Bone-Woman Sing—
Chant Old-Songs—
Song-Memories—
Long-Before-Count—

Wind come—Listen Song—

Wind—Breath—First-of-Things—Listen Song—
Wind—Breath—Last-of-Things—Listen Song—

Wind—come-from-No-Where—
not hurt Sleep of Bones—

*

SANGRE-RUN-FAST

Sangre—Sangre—Sangre—
Young-Girl—run through Forest—like Deer—
Call Name—Young-Wolf—
Call again—

See No-Thing—
Hear No-Thing—only Wind—
Hear Wind in Forest Trees—

Wind-come-from-No-Where—carry—Wolf-Howl—

Young-Child Hear Same Wind—
Same Wind blow Bright-Blood Leaf—
Child born in Same Wind—
Fierce Wind—come-out-of-No-Where—

People not born in Wild Wind—
People Hear Wind—come like Haunt—
Listen—Wind Say—

People not Wolf-Woman— not born in Wild Wind—
People—run—fast—away—

Young-Child Listen Forest—

Hear—far-away—Long-Howl—
Young-Child begin run—

She Know Place—
Place Hombre walk—carry Bag—
carry Noose-Trap—
Place Wind blow Red-Blood Leaf—
Dark-Blood Leaf—
Hombre—Fresh-Blood on Face—
Blood-Fear in Hombre—

Place—Not Carry His Name—

Sangre Breathe Blue-Forest-Flowers—
Breathe in Deep—Blue-Flowers—
Breathe in Deep Smoke-Memory—

He Know This Place—
He Know—must wait—Wolf-Mother come—
Sangre Listen-Trees—Listen-Wind-Speak—
Wind-come-out-of-No-Where—
like Wolf-Mother—
She come-out-of-No-Where—

Sangre Breathe in Deep Feel-Safe Memory—
Breathe Mother Voice—Deep into Him—

Sangre Breathe Blue-Smoke-Memory—
Hold Blue-Forest-Flowers in Memory—
Same Feel-True—like Mist-of-Great-No-Thing—

Wolf-Mother Breathe Sangre—
Breathe Her Breath—Deep into Him—
Deep—so He never Forget—
Breathe She-Wolf Strength into Young-Wolf—
Breathe Blue-Forest-Flowers—
Breathe His Name—

*

Young-Child come—
She—not run so fast—Sangre run fast—
See Young-Wolf—sit—Blue-Forest-Flowers—

Sangre—She Say—

Young-Child—wait—till Breath—come—in—Her—

Sangre—run fast—like Wind—

*

BIG RAIN

Last-Light-Sky—look same like Red-Blood Leaf—
same like Fresh-Blood—
same like Blood from She-Wolf—Die in Trap—
same like Blood-Earth-Place—
Place Blue-Forest-Flowers grow—
Breathe out Blue-Smoke—

Wind-come-from-No-Where—
not come—
Last-Light-Sky—look like Blood—

no Bird Sing—
No-Thing move in Forest—
all Creature Find Safe Place—
Wolf-Woman—Find Safe Place—

Forest Shadow—Air—Sky—all Heavy—
Wind-come-from-No-Where—not come—

Wolf-Woman Find Space in Empty Rock—
Wolf-Woman See—Two-Rocks—
close Place-of-Blue-Flowers—close River—
She sit in Rock-Cave—
wait Big-Rain—

Heavy Rain Wake Woman—Hear Wolf-Howl—
She Look out Cave—all dark—
Rain fall—Hard—Heavy—

Hear—Wolf—Howl—

Hear River-Water—not same River-Sound—
River in hurry—Water rush—

Hear—Wolf—Howl—

Hear Water Splash—

Wolf-Woman run out in Rain—in Black Night—
Wolf-Woman Listen River—
run in Rain—in Black Night—
fall over Branch—
get up—pick up Branch—run more—
Feet in River-Water—
Hear Splash Sound—See Splash in Water—
go Deep Water—
Hold Branch close Splash—
Feel Branch grow Heavy—
Feet Slip—
Strong River-Water take Wolf-Woman—

She Hold Branch—tight—

Branch feel Heavy—

Wolf-Woman—Sudden Pain—Body hit rock—

Branch feel Heavy—

Find other rock—other rock—
Find River-Bank—
pull Hard—long Branch—
pull Hard again—

Branch—Sudden—not Heavy—

Wolf-Woman lie on River-Bank—
not move for tired—
not move for Pain Body—
Rain come down—
River rush—

She-Wolf—Safe—

*

CUERVO NEGRA – BLACK RAVEN

Wolf-Woman sit—Rock-Cave—Work-Medicine—
Wild-Woman make Medicine—
Wound Heal—Pain gone—

Forest Still—no Wind—
where Wind go—

Woman Look Tree—See Black Raven—
Raven on low Branch—not move—Look Woman—
Woman Look down—not good Look Hard—Raven—
Woman Know—
Raven-Eye carry Power-Medicine—
Woman keep Head down—
Look Raven out Side-of-Eye—

Sudden—

Wind come—Wind come—blow Hard—
Wind come—blow Hard—out-of-No-Where—
Forest grow Dark—
Raven fly—Dark-Wind—fly low   Wings wide—
Raven float over Wild-Woman—
float on Dark-Wind—
float like Haunt—

Raven give loud Cry—
Cry sound like many Cry—
like Echo—
like many Echo—
like Haunt—

Wind take Haunt Cry—carry far over Forest—
give Cry to Forest—
give Cry to River—

Wind-from-No-Where—
Wind-not-come-from-Any-Where—
carry Raven-Cry—
to all People—
to all Creature—

Night fall early in Forest—

*

Wolf-Woman—Hear Foot-Step—Hear Wet-Leaf sound—
Night-Spark bright—
Big-Round-in-Sky—have Blood-Face—
Night-Spark—Hang low in Sky—

Wolf-Woman Hide in Rock-Cave-Shadow—
not make sound—

Boots walk close—Cave entrance—Boots Belong—
Hombre—
Same Hombre bring Wolf-Trap—
She Smell—Same Hombre—even She not See Face—
She Smell—Hombre—Soul-Hungry—
She Smell—Hombre—Soul-Starve—
Hombre carry Dark Shadow—
Heavy—
Heavy-as-Black—

Wolf-Woman open Medicine-Bag—
begin mix Medicine—
harm not come—She-Wolf-with-Limp—

Woman Hear Fierce Cry—like Scream—
more Scream—
Raven fly out Night-Spark-Sky—Blood in both Eye—
fly low over Hombre—make Raven-Scream—
Fierce—
Fierce—like Blood—

Hombre begin run—
run fast—
pull hat over Face—
Hold hat both Hand—
Hombre—not See where He go—
Hombre run—

Raven—fly—over—Hombre—
make Raven-Scream—make again—Death-Cry—
make Big Fear in Hombre—

Hombre—Soul-Starve-Smell—
throw Dark Shadow—
Heavy as Black—

Sudden—
Hombre See Blue-Flowers—
See Boot in Blue-Flowers—
Raven gone—Forest quiet—no Wind—

Hombre Look up—
See Blood on Big-Round—make Blood-Light in Forest—
He See Blood-Light on Hand—
He See Blood on Hand—

Big-Round in Sky Send Light—where Blue-Flowers grow—
Hombre See—Blue-Flowers Wake up—
walk out into Forest—

Hombre Boot begin Shake—
Forest Earth begin open—

Hombre See—

White Bones climb out Earth—
many White Bones—

White Bones begin Dance—
make noise—like Clackety-Clack—
White Bones make Dance—close Hombre—
much close—
Hombre not move—

Hombre full Fear—
Fear more—ever He Feel—
White Bones—tear Coat—
White Bones—tear Shirt—
White Bones—make Hole in Chest—

Aaaagh—

Hombre Look in Hole—
He See Blood—
Black Blood—run out Chest—like River—
Black Blood run down Legs—
Boot full Black Blood—

Hombre fall down—He See No-Thing—
He Hear No-Thing—

Big-Round-in-Sky—Face Clear—

Blood all gone—

Big-Round-in-Sky—Walk Over Mountain—

*

LOBA – SHE-WOLF

Wolf-Woman Sit in Rock-Cave—
all dark—Every-Where—
She make Big-Medicine—

Big-Medicine Call Wind-from-No-Where—
She Call—Wind-come-from-No-Where—

Wind-from-No-Where—not come this Place—
not Listen Wolf-Woman—
not Listen Big-Medicine—

Woman Know She-Wolf—Some Place—close Rock-Cave—
Woman Smell She-Wolf—So Strong—
Woman Know in Heart—She-Wolf-with-Limp—
hurt bad—People-hurt—
maybe have Fright Hombre—
now She Fright for Wolf-Woman—

maybe Wolf-Woman look same—like Hombre—

Woman pack Medicine-Bag—Heavy—
Medicine-Bag tell Woman—go Find open Place in Forest—
Sit down—

Woman crawl out Rock-Cave—
Hold Medicine-Bag tight—
She Find open Place—
plenty dark—
She Sit down—

Wind not come—
She-Wolf not come—
not get Medicine—

Medicine-Bag Make-Speak—

Say Woman—not Call Wind-come-from-No-Where—
Say Wolf-Woman—Listen Quiet—Listen Big-Quiet—
Say Woman—Hold Medicine-Bag close Heart—

Say Woman
Sing Wolf-Song all Wolf Know—Before-Count—
Wolf-Song Live in Great Mist—

Woman See Great Mist begin drift—through bare Trees—

all Forest look Soft—

Wolf-Woman Sing Ancient-Wolf-Song—

Ancient-Song—so full Wolf-Woman Breath—
so full Wolf-Woman Heart—
all Forest—full Ancient-Song Wonder—
all Forest—Trees bend down—
Listen Song—

Woman Look up at Sky—
See Big-Round have Bright Face—
See Big-Round Sow Light—like Seeds—all round Wolf-Woman—
Light-Seeds fall on empty Place—
grow bright—
make Big Circle Light—
Light-Seeds fill—all empty Place—

Woman Look down—
See Loba-with-Limp—walk into Circle—
See Loba come lie down—close Medicine-Bag—
Listen end Ancient-Song—

*

RIO – RIVER

River—Old-Before-Know—
Old-Before-Count—
Old—like Begin-Time—

Old—Before People—like Wolf-Woman—
like Hombre—
Before Los Lobos—
Before Tall Trees—

River come—Time of Great Water—
very much Old—beyond Memories—
Same like First River—beyond Memories—

Great-Mystery—She not Same—
Great-Mystery—Not-Come-from-Any-Where—
Great-Mystery—Always—
Great-Mystery—Make Medicine—Make All Thing—

*

Wolf-Woman Sit   Feet in River—
Loba Sit—not far Woman—in bush-Shadow—

River-Water so clear—Woman think—
same like Big-Round—in Night-Sky—

Woman think—
Big-Round—
River—
Old Friend—

Woman bend down—Look in River—
See Woman-Face in River—
Hear Voice Say—

Look Long—
Look Deep—

Woman Look close—See other Face—
See Child-Face—
Woman See—like Sudden—
Child-Face—
Her Face—
same—
other—

where Woman go—

She Sit back—
Look where Loba lie in bush-Shadow—
Loba not under bush—

She See Sangre—

Small-Wolf-Cub—
She Call Name—

Sangre—
Sangre—

He run to Child—
jump in Arms—
He lick Child Face—

Child laugh—
not feel—Wind-come-from-No-Where—
Breathe through Forest—
Leaf make Sound—

Sudden—
Child See Hombre—
Child Hold Sangre—
quick—quick—
She Hide—behind River-Bush—
Hide behind Memory—

*

Wolf-Woman open Eye—take Feet out River—
Call to Loba—Sleep in bush-Shadow—
Loba Sit up—

yawn—
stretch good Back Leg—
Woman—reach—Hand—Loba—

She-Wolf Smell Hand—
Smell Wolf-Woman Hair—
She Smell Woman Feet—
She lie down—Lick Woman Feet—

Woman close Eye—
She not Feel Friend—Touch—
Woman-Tears—wet on Face—
Wild-Woman—
Wolf-Woman—
Woman who Gather-Bones—
Woman—who Sing over Bones—

Wild-Woman—begin Cry—

Soul-Tears—
fall on She-Wolf bad Leg—
wash away Limp—
make Leg whole again—

*

LISTEN – RIVER

not-cloud-Day—
not-Wind—
not-Wind-from-Any-Where—
Big-Shine—hot like Fire in Sky—
Wolf-Woman take off Dress—
hang on Tree Branch—
Shoes under Tree—
Sit on rock—Feet in cool River—

River-Water—all round—make River-Speak—

Woman Listen River-Song—

River-Song Old—
long—long—time—Before People—
River come—long Before-Count—
Wolf-Woman—not Know—Story—

River tell Story in River-Speak—

Woman close Eye—
Listen Song—
both-Ear—

Wolf-Woman Name—

also Wild-Woman—

Wild-Woman Listen—
River make Medicine—
Listen Shine River—
Listen River Sing Ancient-Song—

Woman See She-Wolf—
swim far—
See Loba swim far—Bright River-Shine—
Wind-from-No-Where—not make Shadow—
River get Shine—
Forest get Shine—
All World—
One Thing—

Wolf-Woman slide Body off rock—
She in Deep Water—
Hold Breath—
Sink Slow—
Slow like Big-Shine make Sky red—
before take away Day—
Slow like Die—

Bed of River—
fine-Sand—
River-Water clear—like early morning—

Woman put lazy Fingers in Sand—
Fingers Find round Stone—
not take Stone—
Stone come from Mountain—
one Day look same—
like River-Sand—

*

Sudden—
Woman need Breathe—
Sudden—
fast—
like Fish-Leap—
She come up—
Find Air—
She Breathe in morning Air—
She Breathe in all World—
Wolf-Woman Laugh—

*

Wind-from-No-Where come—
make Wind-Shadow on Water—
Woman stop laugh—
Listen River—
Listen-Shadow-Speak—

River-Shadow Say—
He close Two-Rocks—

Woman Listen—
She not See Him—
not Hear Him—

She Hear—
Song—bring—Dark—like Shadow on Water—
Song like Black Night—
no Night-Spark—
no Big-Round—

*

Sudden—

Wild-Woman Look far up River—
not See—She-Wolf—
River Sudden look—
not same—

Wind—come-from-No-Where—make Shine go Dark—
Wild-Woman Listen Wind—
Listen Dark Song—
Listen Wind-Speak—
Listen Haunt-—

Big Dark—Stay near River—

Wind Say—
Find She-Wolf—Sit on rock—in River—
Big Dark—like—Black Cloud—fall—
Sudden from Sky—
no Light—
Wind-from-No-Where—come—
like Wolf-Howl—
like Haunt—

Wild-Woman Listen Heart—
Listen all Word—

where Loba—
where She-Wolf—

must Find—

*

Wind—come-out-of-No-Where—
one Hear tell of it—
a Whisper—
a Word—
by one who claim Know—

turn away—

this not Wind-from-No-Where—

from one who—Know—
Listen—
Hear—

No-Thing—

Wind—not-come-from-Any-Where—
it come—
Sudden it come—
it come—like Haunt—
a dark Wind—whereof one keep silent—

a Sudden rush of Wind—
dark Wind—come-out-of-No-Where—
dark Shadow on dark Water—

and River—
what She Say—

River Say—

No-Thing—

*

Wild-Woman Know—
Wind-from-No-Where—Breathe on Her—
Wild Breath—Say—
Big-Medicine—wait in Dark Place—
Wild-Woman—Smell Black Medicine—
She Know Smell—
like old Boot—
like Blood-Smell—
like Hombre—

She Feel Dark-Thing—begin happen—in Forest—

Woman Hear Wind-Speak—

Find She-Wolf—
go get Medicine-Bag—
Bad-Thing—happen—Soon—

*

BLUE-FLOWERS – FOREST BONES

Wild-Woman—Many-Eye—Many-Ear—carry Medicine-Bag—

Woman not Know Loba walk hidden path—
not make Sound—in River-Willow—
not See Loba behind rock—

not See—Forest make Dark Shadow—
make Loba same like Shadow—other Eye not See—
not any place—

Wild-Woman—Loba—Stand Still—
both same—
Loba Listen Sound—
Listen Hombre Shout—
Wild-Woman Listen same—

Hombre—
same Hombre—kill Sangre Mother—
Hombre—not See Wild-Woman—
Wild-Woman behind Tree—
She watch Hombre—
He like crazy Man—
Talk bad Spirit—
tear out Blue-Flowers—
Flowers—make Safe—Forest-Bones—
Flowers—Stems—Leaf—Roots—
all get-Break—
He Stamp—

Big Boots Stamp—over Blue-Flowers—
all many get-Break—

*

Blue-Flowers—Blue-Flower-Souls—
where they go—

not this Place—
not other Place—
not any Place—

Light Shine—on—Blue-Flower-Souls—
in Great Mountain Mist—

*

Deep in Dark Earth—
White Bones—Listen Hombre—
Listen Rage Shout—
White Bones—not Fear Hombre—

*

Sudden—
Wild-Woman Stand close Hombre—

where She come—

He not See Her—
then She close—
She Look in Eye—

Hombre want Shout—in Face—
no Shout come—
want hit Woman—Hard—in Face—
Arm not move—
Wild-Woman turn—walk away—

Sudden—

Hombre not See Wild-Woman—

where She go—

*

Hombre begin kick Earth—
Big Boot—kick Blood-Earth—
where Bones lie—

Hombre Listen all thing—
Feel Rage rise in Body—
kick Hard—

kick close to Big-Rock—
He not See—
She-Wolf Stand on Big-Rock—
She-Wolf watch Him—
Yellow-Slit-Eye—
watch—

Hombre Hear Sound—
Look round Him—Hear Sound—
louder—
maybe come from Blood-Earth—
He not Know—
He not See—

Hombre Kneel Down—

begin Dig—

*

PEOPLE-TREE

Hombre Stand up—lean on Big-Rock—
Look up—
Two-Yellow-Eye—Look Him close—

like—
Now—

Stare into Hombre Eye—
Stare into I lim—
Stare through Him—

Hombre Scream—Fright-Scream—
Hombre run—
Big-Fear make Hombre blind—
make Hombre not See where Foot go—
Hombre make fall over Big Root—
People-Tree—reach out Arm—
catch Hombre—
Hold Hombre—tight—

People-Tree make—
Hombre-Breath get bad taste—
Black—shoot out Hombre Mouth—
Black—make Stain on Earth—
Black Breath Stain—
like Rage—
like Poison—

Tree—Hold—Hombre—tight—
no more Scream—

Hombre Face—Red like Blood—
People-Tree let Arm fall—
let Hombre fall—
Hombre—
Big—
Man—
Heavy—
Fall—Big—Heavy—
Breath—all gone—

Hombre—gasp—

Hombre—try—drag—Air—in—Chest—
no Air—
in Hombre Chest—
Lips Speak—
make no Sound—
Eye Big—
Big Fear in Eye—
He Look up—
Lips—Say—no—thing—
no Sound come—

*

Wild-Woman—See—all thing—
Wild-Woman—make Medicine—for Wind—

Wind not wait—
Sudden—Wind come—
Wind come—not-come-from-Any-Where—
Wind come—like Wild Animal—
like Big-Black-Cloud—fight in Sky—
it come—
Wind come—like Black Fright—
like Scream—like Haunt—
Wind come—like—long—long—Wolf—Howl—
like—far—away—it—come—
like far-away—
as Forget—
like Wolf-Howl go High—
go more High—
then fall—
Slow—
Slow—
like—
Die—

Hombre Suck in Deep Breath—

Wind—Listen—Dark Earth—
Deep-Blood-Place—
Listen—Voice—Bones—
Listen Voice Say—

Now—Break—Blood-Word—
Now—Bring—New—Medicine—

Now Speak—Medicine-Woman—
Wild-Woman—

Now Speak—Loba—
She-Wolf—

All Forest Speak—

Hombre—Not Kill Any-More—

Hombre make Black Laugh—
make angry Face—
Hombre Spit—

*

ANCESTORS

Wild-Woman Step over—Line-After-Count—

Same like Line-Before-Count—

Stand in Country—
Ancient-Yellow-Bones—

Wild-Woman not Hear—in all Remember—
Such Medicine-Wind—

Soft-Touch—like Close Tears—
like Haunt-Echo—
like Ancient-Wind—

it come—
like Wind-come-out-of-No-Where—
like Wind-that-Breathe—
over—
Great Water—

First-Wind—Float—in—Stillness—
Wild-Woman—Listen—Great Stillness—

Wind-from-No-Where—
Say—
Ancient-Yellow-Bones—Make-Pattern—

Wind-from-No-Where—
Hold—

Breath—
make—Big—Hush—

Sudden—
All World—Make Open—
Wild-Woman—
never See—so many—Bones Know-Pattern—

some Pattern so Big—
not Know—
how—so-Big—Creature—walk—
Big—Heavy—Bones—

Wind-from-No-Where Show—
follow me—
Wind Show—
go—Find Hombre—

First Steps—Ancient-Yellow-Bones—
take—
over—Count-Line—

*

RE-MEMBER

Bones—Remember—All—Thing—
Remember—same like—Re-Member—
and not same—
Bone-Ash—Bone-Dust—Scatter by Wind
Make-Pattern—

Wind Know—
Bones Know—

Ancient-Yellow-Bones Say—
many Yellow Bones—Not-Know-Pattern—

Bones Not Make-Pattern—
Not Sleep—

need one Hombre—
maybe this Hombre—

maybe He Know-Pattern—

maybe—He Find Bones—
Not-Make-Pattern—
same like He Know—
maybe—He—Make-Pattern—good—

many Bones here—Not-Know-Pattern—
same—like Him—
Not Whole—Not See-Pattern—

maybe Hombre—Find first Ancestor—
Him Not Sleep—
Him angry—

Find all—Not Whole—same—like Him—
maybe—He Find Break-in-Pattern—in Old Ancestor—
maybe He Make Old Ancestor Whole—
all—Bones—Sudden—Make—Pattern—same—

*

LINE-AFTER-COUNT

Hombre—refuse—
cross—
Line-After-Count—

Hombre Make Big Curse—
Hombre Say Bad Spell—
Hombre Spit—
Hombre—get—Big—Rage—

Hombre—kick—Stone—
Big Animal-Skin Boot—

Hombre—not—move—
not—one—Step—
Hombre Face Red—
Red—like She-Wolf Blood—
Red—like Blood Spill on Sangre—
Blood-Red like Fall-Leaf in Forest—
Bright-Red like She-Wolf Blood—on Fall-Leaf—

Wolf-Woman pick up kick-Stone—put in Medicine-Bag—

how get Hombre cross—
Line-After-Count—

Wild-Woman close Eye—Look in Dream-Cave—

See Line-Pattern—See First-Wind—
Listen—First—Stillness—
First-Wind—move over Great Still Water—
First-Wind—come-from-No-Where—
Breath-of-All-Things—

Woman—Hold Head both Hand—

Listen Wind-Speak—

White Bone Know—Find—way—

Wild-Woman—Sit down—
open Medicine-Bag—
take—White Bone—

Wild-Woman Find Bone—close River—
not Find other Bones—
She keep Bone—
one Day—Find all Bones—Make-Belong—
Make-Pattern—

Wild-Woman Hold Bone—
Touch—Place—Dream—Eye—

She begin rock—

She See—Dream-Hombre-Face—
She See—All of Him—

She put Bone in front Hombre-Dream-Face—
She Smack Hand in Hombre Face—
She Show Hombre—Two Hand—

Woman put Bone—
balance—

one Hand—

balance—
other Hand—

make Bridge—
make Cross-Place—

Woman close Dream-Eye—

*

BEFORE-COUNT

Wild-Woman Sing Song—
Old Song—

all Story-Teller—Know Song—since Child—
Song Call up all Bones—
all Bones sleep close this Song—
all Bones sleep—even foot walk far—
all Know Song—

Song tell Hidden Bones—
take Hombre—

cross Line-After-Count—

Song Call up many—many—Bones—

Song ask—
Bones Make-Pattern—
walk behind Hombre—
make much Bone-Talk—make Big-Clackety-Clack—
Show Smile Teeth—Big Teeth—Sharp Teeth—
Make-Scare Hombre—

Hombre Hear—Big Noise—
Hombre get Fright—like Hombre jump out Skin—
Hombre Run—
Sound like many Feet—He Run so fast—
not See Line-After-Count—
not See He cross Line—
not See Bones make Trick on Him—

Song finish—
Wild-Woman—put White Bone—
Medicine-Bag—
White Bone—close by—Stone—
Wild-Woman Listen—
Listen—

Listen—it come—

Wind-out-of-No-Where—
it come Naked—
it come—Restless—
like Wake-Up—out-of-No-Where—
it make Sound like—
Old-Know—
like—
never Hear—Beyond-Count—

like—
come out Ancient-Memories—
like—
Make Big Fright—

Hombre—Listen—
Wind—Moan—low—over—ground—

Listen—
Wind-Speak—
like—Rattle—dead—Branches—

Listen—
like—Clackety-Clack—

Listen—
like—dry—White—Bones—
Re-Member-Pattern—

*

White Bones turn—
go back Forest—quick-quick—
go back—
Big-Rock—
go—Deep—Pattern-Sleep—

*

NOT-SEE-TRICK

Hombre angry—

angry—
like Fire-Mountain—
angry—
like Black-Cloud—
angry—
like Storm-Sky—
angry—
like Fire-Snake—

like—Big Flash make Night look Day—
He Shout—Angry—

He not See Trick—

Wild-Woman—take Hombre—meet—
Ancient-Yellow-Bones—
He meet—
Not-Sleep—Ancient-Yellow-Bones—
Bones—
all Animal—
all People—
all kind Yellow Bones—
all Not Sleep—
All Not Find-Pattern—

Hombre meet angry Man—Bones—Not Make-Pattern—

Man rattle Bones—hit Bone on Bone—make Big Noise—

try hit Hombre—loose Leg Bone—

He—try—Stand—
loose Leg—
Hang—
down—

so many Bones—Not—Find-Pattern—

Man big tired—

Man—stop—try—move—
Man Bones lie on ground—Not Find-Pattern—

Hombre bend over—Look close—all Bones—
He move many Bones—

Hombre Find Bone in bad Place—angry Place—
He make good Place—Bone fit in good Place—

*

Hombre Face change—He not look Same Hombre—
Hombre Face—Strange—

*

He Look close—Find Big-Trouble Bone—
He See Angry-Bone—
near end—
many Spine-Bones—

He Kneel down—
He tell Bones—Not-Find-Pattern—
lie still—
Hombre come—make good Place—

Hombre Hand take Small Bone—

Small Bone—face other way—in Spine—
Hombre Hold Bone in Hand—

He Speak—Other-Word—to Bone—
He Speak—many Other-Word—

Hombre close Eye—

Slow—He turn Bone—
Slow—Bone look same like all Bones—
Hombre make Bone fit—

Hombre need other Hand—same like Hombre Hand—
He See Wild-Woman—
He Show open Hand—
Wild-Woman take Hand—
She Make Tears fall—on Small Bone—

Hombre—still not finish—
need make Heal—loose Leg Bone—
Hombre ask Wild-Woman help make Heal—

Wild-Woman take Hand full Clay-Soil—mix full Woman
Tears—
white paste—make new Leg-Bend—
put Leg in lap—begin rock—
begin Sing—

Song—tell—

how—Pattern—Hold—Break-Piece—

Break-Piece—Make-Learn—
Share Learn—whole Body—

Woman finish Song—make Bow to Hombre—

Hombre take Woman Hand—make Bow to Woman—

Woman—full many Tears—

Hombre Work finish—
watch Man-Bones on ground—
See All-Man-Bones—Make-Pattern—
Find—Sleep—in—cool—dark—Earth—

*

FIND-PATTERN

Wild-Woman—She-Wolf—Hombre—
Stand—Look—Line-Before-Count—

same Line also Name—Line-After-Count—

Wild-Woman Feel Ancient-Power—
Feel Ancient-Wind—same Wind—come-from-No-Where—
Wild-Woman Hear Ancient-Voices—

Voices-Live-in-Wind—

Wind-come-from-No-Where—Breathe through Ancient-
People—

Ancient-Ones not ask—where Wind come from—
not ask where Tree come from—
not River—
not Great Water—

Wild-Woman Hear—Ancient-Song—
Song that Wind carry—
come through Mist-of-Great-No-Thing—
come from so long away—
carry Voice Ancient-People—

where they gone—maybe Bones—
Count Begin—
Line change Name—
Wild-Woman Feel Tears—

who Sing over Bones—
no People—
no Voices—

maybe Wind Sing—
Wind-come-from-No-Where—
Wind Sing over Bones—
like Haunt—like Voices Sing—
so—far—away—Feel—like—Dream—

Big Dream fly on Wind—come-from-No-Where—
Big Dream fly through Ancient-Mist—
Wind carry Big Dream—through Dark Night—
no Big-Round—
fly slow over Sleep-People—
leave Dream-Story—
leave Memories—
leave Dream—where Ancient-Ones go—

maybe we leave—one Day—
same like Them—
make walk—Great-Ancient-Mist—

*

Hombre walk Bare-Foot—He carry Animal-Skin Boots—
not want Skin Boots—

not want kick—
not want hurt—
any-thing—
not want hurt—
any-one—
any-more—
not want Name—
Hombre—

He ask Wild-Woman—what He do—
where put Skin Boots—
Wild-Woman Look Sky—
See Big Storm-Cloud—grow dark—
Wild-Woman Say—throw Boots into Sky—
Wind—take—Boots—

Hombre throw Boots—High as Tall Tree—Cloud-High—
Wind make Skin Boots walk Sky—
make Boots kick Storm-Cloud—
make Rain fall—
Hard Rain—
Wind blow Rain—
other place—

Hombre not believe Eye—
how Wind make Boots—kick Cloud—
make Rain—

He Look Wild-Woman—
how She Know—Wind do this thing—

Wild-Woman Look Him—She Say—
Wind-come-from-No-Where—
one Hear tell of it—
a Whisper—
a Word—
by one who claim Know—

turn away—
this not Wind-from-No-Where—

from one—who Know—
Listen—
Hear—

No-Thing—

Wind—not-come-from-Any-Where—
it come—
Sudden—it come—
it come—like Haunt—
a dark Wind—
whereof one keep silent—
a Sudden rush of Wind—dark Wind—

come-out-of-No-Where—
dark Shadow on dark Water—

and River—
what She Say—

River Say—

No-Thing—

*

Hombre Look Wild-Woman—
He Look—Soft-Eye—
Many Tears—
Say—He want throw Name—
up in Sky—
same like Boots—
no more Hombre—
want new Name—

Wild-Woman tell Hombre—
Sit—
She Look Medicine-Bag—
She take out White Bone—
give White Bone—Man-with-No-Name—

Woman Say—take White Bone—close River—
close Blue-Flowers—
close Big-Rocks—
close Place Bones Make-Sleep—

walk up—down—River—All Day—
All Night—
ask Big-Round in Night-Sky—
make Light—
very bright—
ask Night-Sparks—
come close—come close River—
make Shine—White Bones—
even same—this White Bone—

Man-with-No-Name—Hold White Bone High—
Bone Call—in Voice-of-Belong—
Bone Call in Talk He Know—

come to me—
come Talk Man-who-have-No-Name—
come Talk Wild-Woman—
She have much Power—
come—all Lost Bones—
Make-Pattern—

Wild-Woman—Look Man-with-No-Name—
She—Say—Man-with-No-Name do this—
Bones Make-Pattern—go Sleep in dark Earth—
New Name come Find Man—

*

ALONE

all way walk back River—
Man-with-No-Name—pick up Stones—
Man-with-No-Name—
put Stones in Coat pockets—
put Stones in Bag—
many Stones—so many—not count—
Heavy—

Man-with-No-Name—wet-hot—
He taste Salt—burn dry Mouth—
Lips crack—Salt Sting—
Bag full Stones—Heavy—
Man-with-No-Name—get Blood on Hand—
Blood from Heavy Bag—
cut this Hand—
cut other Hand—

Man-with-No-Name—
not See Wild-Woman—
not See She-Wolf—
maybe go other way—

why not Say—

Man-with-No-Name Feel like—not other People—
any Place—
not help carry Stones—

Man-with-No-Name—See Blood on Feet—

Touch Face—

See Blood on Hand—

many bush have—Thorns—

Man-with-No-Name—get Deep Wound—

He Cry out—

Who Hear Cry—

*

Dark Forest—no Big-Round in Sky—
Man-with-No-Name—come close River—
make empty—Bag of Stones—
make empty all pocket—

Man-with-No-Name take off clothes—

walk in River—

River-Water Feel like Friend—

He let go—

sink to River-Bed—soft River-Sand—

Man-with-No-Name—Feel—like River flow through Him—

River-Water feel like many Tears—

so many Tears—all His Tears—

He Feel—
River wash away all Blood—
make clean—Deep Thorn-Wound—

Man-with-No-Name—Rise-Up from River-Bed—

Find new Breath—wait—

Man-with-No-Name—

Breathe in Dark Forest Night—

Breathe in Alone—

*

STONE LISTEN STORY

Early Morning—Forest quiet—
Man-with-No-Name—make—Big Circle Stones—
Place Listen—River-Speak—

He Hold White Bone—High up—all Stone See White Bone—

He Sit Centre—
not Know what come—
perhaps Stone Know—
He turn—make Face Look—all Side—

Man Speak—
Make all Stone welcome—
tell Stone—what Man must do—

first—
Man must tell—all Bad Story—

Man Say—
He make many Trap—Kill Wolf—
He tell all Story—
He tell Blood-of-Story—

He tell how Wind come like Storm—
blow Leaf—
look same Big-Shine—
blow Leaf—
look same Storm—
Leaf full Blood—
come from She-Wolf—Man catch in Trap—

Wind blow Blood-Leaf—in Man Face—
He taste She-Wolf Blood—

never Forget—

He make She-Wolf get—long—slow—Pain—

never end—

never end—

long—slow—Death—

Man—want tell Stones—

He Feel She-Wolf Pain—
now in Man-Heart—
He carry Her Pain—
always—

Also carry Strong She-Wolf-Face—
in Heart—
always—

He Say—

Not—Kill—ever—again—

Man-with-No-Name Say—more Bad Story—

He tell—Black Raven put Fear into Man—

He tell—

all Bones Dance—Clackety-Clack—
Bones make tear in Shirt—
make Deep Hole Man Chest—
Man See Blood—
Black Blood—

He get Horror inside Him—

He See Blue-Flowers—many Blue-Flowers—
leave Place in Soil—walk away in Forest—

He Say—

He See—Black Blood—come out Chest—like River—
make Black-Blood-Pool in Forest—

Man-with-No-Name—tell last Story—

He tell Stones—He think He go Mad—
He Dig up Bones—
He Stamp all Blue-Flowers—

Sudden—
Big She-Wolf come—make Big Fright on Him—

not—Know—other—thing—

*

He Make-Peace for Ancient-Bones—
Bones have Same Angry—
like He Know—

He not Feel Angry—

He Feel some Hard Thing—make Heavy in Chest—
not Know what it Say—not Know Name—
He Listen—what come Speak—

*

WHITE BONE

White Bone begin Shake in Man-Hand—
Shake so Hard—
Call up Wind—
Wind-come-from-No-Where—
Wind-from-No-Where—make Big Noise—
All Forest Know Wind come—

Wind blow Stones—
all Stones Make-Pair—
all Pair Stones—Find Place—
in Big Circle round Blue-Flowers—
round Sleep Bones—

Wind-from-No-Where—not blow Last Stone—
Last Stone—not have Pair—
Last Stone—Stay—
same place—

Wind-come-from-No-Where—
blow Trees—
blow Shadow on River—
blow Forest Dust—
High in Air—up into Blue-Sky—

Wind-from-No-Where—make Storm-Cloud—
make Boot kick Dark-Cloud—
make Rain fall—

Rain fall on Man-with-No-Name—
Rain fall on Small Stone—

Small Stone lie in front Man—
Small Stone—not have Pair—

Wind-from-No-Where—blow Hard—
White Bone fly out Man-Hand—
White Bone begin beat—
on Chest—
Man-with-No-Name—

White Bone beat Hard—Look Hole in Man-Chest—
Hole—Make by Clackety-Clack—Dance Bones—
close—
Black Blood make Big Pool in Forest—

White Bone Find Hole in Chest—make new Sound—
hit Hard Thing—
Hole in Chest—open—not Heal—
Hard Thing—not move—

White Bone hit more Hard—more fast—
Wind—come-out-of-No-Where—
come blow—
blow where White Bone beat—

Small Black Stone fall out Hole—
fall out Man-Heart—
Hole close—
leave
Memory-Mark—

Man not Forget this—

Sudden—
Rain blow Other-Where—

Man-with-No-Name—pick up two Stones—
Hold both same—both not same—

one Black Stone—come out Heart—
one White Stone—no Pair—
Pair Stone—come—

two Stone—Live—close—
Black Stone—White Stone—
each Belong other—

Man Look—Clear Eye—
He See—Both One Stone—

*

NOT WANT KNOW

Man-with-No-Name—
Look close—

Long Bone He Hold—

what do Bone look like—maybe Leg—
Bone not thick—not Heavy—
maybe Fox—
Man Shake Head—not Fox—

Man not want remember—
all Animal—
caught in Trap—

not want think—
Animal Pain—
bite Leg—
leave Leg in Trap—
maybe Live—maybe Die—
Free—

not She-Wolf—Mother Sangre—She not get away—

Man-with-No-Name close Eye—
He Call Memory—come Talk what happen—

Memory make See-in-Head—

Place up-Stream—Man set Trap—
come back—empty Trap—

much Blood—

He Know Place—well—
Man begin walk—follow River—
not where River go—Great Water—
He go other way—
keep Look—Mountain—
go Find—River-Place—Big-Rocks—
Place—rocks cross River—
not good Foot-Cross-Place—
Big Rain come—
River flood—
not Safe—

Man Feel tired—inside—

Small-Voice Say—
Not Want Know—

Voice Want Say—
Turn Round—
Go Back—

Not Look Rocks—

Not Look River—

*

RIVER CROSS-PLACE

Man sit rock—near River—
Hand in pocket—Touch two Stone—

Touch two Stone—Man Feel better—

He make Memory—See Small Pool—
Water go round-round—fast—
He make Memory—Steep Side Pool—
Big care—not fall in—
Man Feel cold Fright—
begin step—rock—other rock—
See—Small—Pool—

He turn back—
He turn back—

He not turn back—

*

Man-with-No-Name Know—

No-Thing undo this—
Man sit on rock—
He Weep—

He Weep—so many Tears—

He not let Tears come out—
whole Life—

No Word—No Speak—Ever Take This From Him—
This Belong Him—For All Life—

Man Say Blood-Promise-Words—

Man take off Coat—
roll up Sleeve—
lie down—
begin Gather-Bones—out Water—

Bones that go round-round—
round—
never end—
never end—

*

He Know—what not there—what not in Water—

He Look all Side Pool—

far Side—rock make small crack—
He See Long White Bone—catch in crack—
same like Wolf-Woman give Him—

He Know—what He not See—
He Know—not Find—not on rock—

He Know—
two Foot gone—

two Foot Haunt Him—

Now—

Now—

Now He Know—
He Look Bones—
Bones tell Him—

Lobo—Die—This—Place—
Lobo—not have—good Leg—
Man Look close—

Strong Skull—

Mouth wide open—
Pain-Howl—

Man Know—Howl—with Him—
inside Him—
Not leave Him—
Not now—
Not any other now—

Man-with-No-Name—
take off loose Shirt—wrap all Bones—
Safe—
Skull—rest—on top—

Man still search—not here—
not See other here—
maybe gone all way—
Great Water—

Man-with-No-Name think—
maybe not Find—two Foot—
maybe Lobo—Not Make-Pattern—

Man-with-No-Name—Know—
He always carry—
Big Heavy—
in Heart—

MAN ASK HELP

Man sit—Hold Knife—Belong Father—
Father Die—He give Son Knife—
Big Sign—Son—Man—

He make good Work—
Knife Know—many good Work—

Man-with-No-Name—sit Soft Forest Leaf—
He lean—rest Back—Big Leg of Tree—
All Tree in Forest—only One Leg—
Tree not have Foot—
not walk—

Man Dig—Dig down Tree-Leg—
not Find Foot—
Man Find—
many long Finger—

He ask Tree—
Say Yes—
Man cut two piece Finger—

make two Foot—
Lobo need two Foot—Make-Pattern—

Big Forest Tree Say—Yes—

Man-with-No-Name—Lake Knife—Belong Father—
Hold—Big-Sign-Knife—
make—two—Lobo—Foot—

He—put two Foot Same—
all White Bones—

maybe—Lobo—Make—Pattern—
maybe Lobo Find—Sleep—in cool Earth—
maybe He Sleep—Place-of-Blue-Flowers—

*

HELP MAKE-PATTERN

Man-with-No-Name—
Find Wild-Woman—Find She-Wolf—
Sit—Speak—Blue-Flowers—
Sit—Speak—White Bones—

Blue-Flowers—Make-Welcome—White Bones—
Know White Bones—Belong Forest—

Man—untie—Shirt—take—out—Bones—
take one—take other one—
take all other one—

Show Wild-Woman—one Bone—one Place—

all—Bones—rest—on—Forest—Leaf—
all White Bones—

two Foot—
Knife make—out Forest-Wood—
close White Bones—

Man-with-No-Name—not Breathe—
not Know—He make good Foot—
not—Know—Bones—Make—Pattern—

*

Sudden—

Wind come—
Wind-come-from-No-Where—

Wind come like Storm—
Wind come through Forest—make all Trees—toss Head—
make all Leaf on ground—fly like Bird—
make River Sing—loud Song—
Bright—Dark—both same—

Wind—from-No-Where—
Sudden—
make Stillness—
all thing—make quiet—

Trees—
not—
move—

White Bones—Slow—begin—Re-Member—

Slow—begin—Make-Pattern—

Slow—Step in Wood Foot—first Leg—
Slow—Step in Wood Foot—other Leg—

Slow—begin—Stand—

Slow—begin—Dance—

*

GO FIND NAME

Man-with-No-Name walk—slow—Forest—
He Look in Head—

where—Man—Find—Name—

Name not in Head—
Name not sit on log—
not no-where—out-there—
not—far-away—
Name—not Hide—

Man think—He not want Name—
all Name—mean Some Story—
Man change—Name not change—
Man carry old Name—like Heavy—

what Name not change—

Great Mist—not change—
Big-Round in Night-Sky—change—not change—

Man close Eye—try See new Name—
He not See—Name—

Man—Stand Still—
put Hand in pocket—
put Hand in other pocket—
both Hand make Find—

Man Look—one pocket—White Stone—
Man Look—other pocket—Black Stone—

He Laugh—

He Know—Name Look Him—in Face—
why He not Hear Name—
maybe come—other time—

Man so busy—Look in Head—
not See other Stone on ground—

Man trip—
Man fall—

He lie on ground—Look other Stone—

Man Know—Name—not this other Stone—

Sudden—

Man drop Stone—
New Name—not Stone—

He Know He Say Word—
many time—

Other—

Other—

He sit up—
Sudden—He full—Happy—

He Shout New Name—loud—like All Forest Hear—

Other—

He Shout—again—

more loud—

Other—

Other—

Wind come—
Wind-from-No-Where—come catch Shout—
Wind catch Name—

Other—

Wind-from-No-Where—carry Name—all over Forest—
Wolf-Woman sit close—Blue-Flowers—
Listen on Wind—

She-Wolf—close Wolf-Woman—Look up—
Listen—Strange Sound in Wind—

all Forest—
all River—
all Mountain—
Listen New Name—

Rocks—Water at Source—
Listen New Name—

Wind-come-from-No-Where—
carry New Name—High—
all way—High—Big-Blue—
all way—Big-Shine—

Man sit on Forest ground—

He Laugh—
He Weep—many Tears—
He Weep—

Man—whole—Body—Feel—like—Break—
He Sob—till Body—not more Tears—
till Body—Feel—Heavy-Weep-Pain—

Memory come Show Him—all Dead Animal in Trap—
many Trap—He set in Forest—

He Look Face—
this Dead Face—
He Look so many Face—
so many Dead Face—
He Look every Dead Face—
many—time—

He Look so many Dead Eye—Light all gone Eye—
He—take Light away—Eye—
how can Man Live—
so many Dead Face—
Dead Eye—
Haunt Man—

Man Look—His two Hand—This Two Hand—

Make so much Dead—

Man make Deep Blood-Word—put Hand—Heart-Place—
Man Feel Deep Heart-Pain—
like He Not Know—
like He Not ever Know—
Heart Weep—many Tears—
Man—Feel—Heart—Break—
Man—Feel—Deep—Heart—Wound—

Man Know Heart-Wound—Not Heal—

Not Ever—

Man bow Head—

He—Say—

Yes—

Other—Live—Always—Break-Heart—

*

BLOOD OFFER

Wild-Woman—Other—Sit Talk—
She-Wolf lie—half-Sleep—keep watch—Medicine-Bag—
Listen Voice—make She-Wolf Feel good—

Woman tell Other—
want Make-Offer to All-Thing—

Woman Sweep Ground—Clean—
Draw Big Circle Line—

Draw Straight Line—cut Circle—

make top empty Place—
make bottom empty Place—

Woman Say—top Light—
Woman Say—bottom Dark—

She Show Place—Big-Shine—come out of Dark—

Big-Shine climb over top of Circle—
Slide down other Side—Fall into Dark—
all below Straight-Line—Big Dark—

Big-Shine Look for Light—all Dark Place—

Find Light again—Place Dark end—

take Big-Shine—
All Day—All Night—do this—

Wolf-Woman draw line for River—
top of River—
She Show Water at Source—
bottom River—
Big Space—

Wolf-Woman not Know how Great Water look—

She draw many Tree—make Forest—
Woman draw Place—Sad-Grass—Sing—
She draw Mountain—place Big-Round go Hide—

She make Line-Before-Count—also Name Line-After-Count—

both-same—both-not-same—

Woman fetch White-Sand—
make White Mist—many place—
keep all People Safe—

*

Woman Sit open Space—make Small Fire—
blow Fire—make it grow—
Place—Offer—Over—Fire—

Woman take Knife—
Make Small Cut on Hand—
Blood on Finger—make Blood-Mark—Place-Between-Eye—
take Hand full Earth—
pour on Head—
take Water Gourd—
wash away Earth—like Rain—

*

Woman raise both Arm—
Offer Thank—

She-Wolf—Sit up—Listen Woman-Speak—

Woman Offer—Thank—
All—Tree—Bush—Rock—Cave—
Thank—Bones Make-Pattern—
Thank—Bones Not Make-Pattern—
Thank—Blue-Flowers—
grow Big—like Field—
Thank—all Animal—Bird—
Live in Forest—

Woman—turn—Look River—
Hold Hand on Heart—
Woman—Speak—
Ancient-Thank—for—River—

She turn—Speak River—

She Say—
Wild-Woman—Other—She-Wolf—
go—Leave—Forest—
go—Source—

River Say—

No-Thing—

*

Sudden—
Wind-from-No-Where—come—
like Fierce—
like Black Raven—
Wind make Big Dust Circle in Forest—
make Day go Dark—
make Big Wave on River—make River go Wild—

River—Water—begin—run—both—way—
make—Feel—all—Thing—
gone—Lost—Pattern—
Wind-from-No-Where—
lift—Medicine-Bag—
High—in Air—

Wild-Woman Stand up—run catch Medicine-Bag—

Wind-come-from-No-Where—make Bag fly—
much High for Woman—

She jump—one time—one other time—
one last time—

Woman jump So High—Other afraid for Woman—
Other afraid—She fly away in Wind—
Other—Sudden get Fright—
He not See Woman again—
Other not wait—
He Jump up—
catch Bag—
catch Woman—

Wind-come-from-No-Where—
Know how blow down Forest—Big Tree—
Know how make River run up Mountain—

Wind-from-No-Where—do All Many Thing—

Wind-from-No-Where—
not take Wolf-Woman—
out Arms—
Other—

*

WIND SAY LISTEN HEART

Wolf-Woman Sit on Ground—
She have Bag of Stones—each Stone—not Same—

Woman have Big Ask—
need make Ground flat—need draw wide Mark-on-Ground—
need draw Line-Story—

*

Wolf-Woman Stand—
walk round Mark-on-Ground—
She Look Mark—
not Touch—

Woman take Bag Small Stone—
All Stone come—other place—
not two Stone look Same—
not have Same Voice—
Woman Say Word over—
this Stone—

this Stone—

all Stone get Word—

all Stone—put in Basket-for-Throw—

She take Basket—
Hold over Mark-on-Ground—
throw-All-Stone—

one Stone—

not stay inside Line—Mark-on-Ground—

one Stone—roll—far—
not-Know-Place—

*

Other sit close She-Wolf—Side River—
Other Listen River-Water—not Know River-Speak—
Other have much Talk-in-Heart—
many Voice—all Talk Same—

She-Wolf not think—

She-Wolf Know—Big Make-Change happen—

She Smell Wolf-Woman—
Smell not-Same—

She-Wolf Listen Wind—
Wind not-Same—

*

She-Wolf—Know—Stone-Speak—

She Know all thing Change—

She-Wolf lift Head—make Long—Long—Howl—

*

WIND COME

Wind-from-No-Where—come—Slow—
make Same Long Howl—Same like She-Wolf—
Wind in Trees—make—Howl—
River-Water—make Howl—come—out—Dark—Wave—

All—Forest—Listen—
All—Creature—Listen—
All—Bird—Listen—
All—Bones Make-Pattern—rise—out—Dark—Earth—
Listen—

*

Listen—

from—Mountain—Source—all—way—Great Water—
not—one—Sound—

Wind—Sudden—Still—

*

She-Wolf Stand—

Turn away—

begin—Slow—walk—into—Forest—

Not—Look—Back—

*

BLOOD-WORD

Wild-Woman Gather all Stone—
from Mark-on-Ground—
not two Stone Same—
put in Bag—

not Find—
Stone—roll—other way—

Wild-Woman—
Speak Offer over—Mark-on-Ground—
Kneel—
Make Ground Smooth—both Hand—
Other—Stand close—Hold—
Medicine-Bag—

Wild-Woman—Other—Begin Long Walk—

Make—Leave—Forest—

Not—Look—Back—

*

CUT FREE CORD

Wild-Woman Heart Heavy—Hold many Tear—
Other—take Woman Arm—
Find good Place—
sit—
rest—

Wild-Woman need make—Cut-Free-Cord—
need make—Tears like Rain—

need make—Speak-Offer—She-Wolf—

Wild-Woman take Knife—Medicine-Bag
Gather—long Grass—make thick-twist Cord—

Woman Stand close River—Cut Cord—One—Clean—Cut—

Gather all Piece Grass—
Hold—close—Heart—
Feel Heart—
Break—

taste—Blood in Throat—
begin Weep—many Tears—
Tears fall—same like Storm-Rain—

Wild-Woman Stand in Water—cover Knee—
Cast all Grass on Shine-River—

Chant—Word—
many time—

many—time—

Word mean—

Keep Safe—

Keep Safe—

Keep Safe—

*

Other—watch—
sit on log—
He Say No-Thing—

He watch Woman—take off Dress—
Slow—
take off Shoes—
Slow—
watch Woman walk in River—
Slow—

watch Wild-Woman—go Deep River-Water—

not See Woman—

Wild-Woman—River—both—Same—

*

DEEP RIVER CALL WOMAN

Wild-Woman Feel River-Pull—go River-Journey—
all way—Great Water—

River tell Woman—

Great Water—so Big—
Woman Look—Woman Look—Woman Look—
ever—so—many—time—
Great Water—never end—

Woman Feel Chest Cry—
Not Breath—
Not Breath—

Need—Breathe—
Not—time—think—
Make—Move—Now—

Wild-Woman Break Shine-Water—
take Big Breath Forest Air—
Listen Forest take Big Breath—
Listen—Wind-come-from-No-Where—
Speak—

Fierce Wind-Speak—
Say—
put Dress—
put Shoe—
go fetch Medicine-Bag—
Find Stone—roll off Pattern-in-Earth—

Listen—two Ear—

what it Say—

*

Stone Say—

She-Wolf now Free—
She-Wolf now Live full Wolf-Story—

Woman now Free—
Woman now Live full Woman-Story—

Wild-Woman—Other—Free—Leave Forest—

*

ANCIENT STORY – GREAT MIST

People Say—Story float on Great Mist—
Not want Forget Most-Only-Truth—

Story So Old—
People Know Story—Before-Count—
After-Count—People Not Know—

Wind-from-No-Where—Know All Story—
Know All Animal-Story—
Know All Animal-Speak—

Animal—run fast—tell Story—
Speak with Feet—

Big Animal—Heavy—
Speak—Long Nose— Big Tusk—

many Speak Voice—like She-Wolf Howl—

many Bird Story—Live-Speak like Wind—

*

Wind—come-out-of-No-Where—
one Hear tell of it—
a Whisper—
a Word—
by one who claim Know—

turn away—
not Wind-from-No-Where—

from one—who Know—
Listen—

Hear—

No-Thing—

Wind—not-come-from-Any-Where—
it come—
Sudden it come—
it come—like Haunt—
a dark Wind—
whereof one keep silent—

a Sudden rush of Wind—
dark Wind—come-out-of-No-Where—
dark Shadow on dark Water—
and River—
what She Say—

River Say—

No-Thing—

*

Animal—Not-Make-Count—

Animal keep Story Strong—
All Animal Live Story—

*

People come from Place call—Deep-Belong—
Deep-Belong People—Tell Story—
Carve-Pattern-in-Rock—
Dance—
Deep-Belong-People—
Make-Pattern—with Heart-Eye—

Deep-Belong-People—
Not-Make-Count—

what happen—make People lose Heart-Eye—

Make-Count Start—not Heart-Eye—
People not Dance—not Tell Story—
People get lost in Count—
People Forget Deep-Belong—

Slow—
People begin walk into Great Mist—

*

Great Mist come—
come gentle—like Soft Breath—

Wind-from-No-Where—
carry Deep-Belong Story—
float—on—top—Great Mist—

*

GREAT MIST STORY

Not one Know—when Story first Speak—
only Wind-from-No-Where—
Know this—
Wind-from-No-Where—
and Source—

Story Tell—

if—
two People—
Both-One See Light-of-Source in other—
Both-One See in other—Heart—Make—Pattern-of-Fire—
Both-One—Make-Source-Pattern—with Full Heart—
Both-One See in other—Shine Place—

more Beautiful-True—Any-Know-Thing—
if—
two People—
Both-One Have Shine Face—like Child—
Both-One See Shine Place in other—
Both-One Make-Offer—Over Source-Water—
Both-One Make-Offer—with Full Heart—
Both-One Make-Offer—Open Hand—
Both-One See Face—and Face of other—
in—Clear—Still—Water—

Sudden—

Wind-come-from-No-Where—
Lift—Both-One—Over—Still—Water—
into—Place Deep-Belong—
into—Great Mist Story—

*

People want Know—what lie other Side—Still Water—

Only Source Know—
Only Source—and Wind—
Wind-come-from-No-Where—
Know This—

*

Wind—
come-out-of-No-Where—

one Hear tell of it—

a Whisper—
a Word—

by one who claim Know—

turn away—
this not Wind-from-No-Where—

from one—who Know—
Listen—
Hear—

No-Thing—

*

Wind—
not-come-from-Any-Where—

it come—

Sudden it come—
come—like Haunt—

a dark Wind—
whereof one keep silent—

a Sudden rush of Wind—
dark Wind—
come-out-of-No-Where—
dark Shadow—
on dark Water—

and River—
what She Say—

River Say—

No-Thing—

Raven Fly Forest—float on black Wings—
float on Wind—come from-No-Where—
now See—now not See—Raven—
Raven fly through Mist-of-Great-No-Thing—
Float on soft Wind—come-from-No-Where—
All Forest look like Mystery—

Raven Look down—
See Place of Two Rocks—
See Misty Blue-Flower clearing—
Smell smoke in Air—come from Blue-Flowers—
Raven See Wolf-Woman—sit close She-Wolf—

He turn—
Fly low over Blue-Flowers—
Look for She-Wolf—
Look for Wolf-Woman—

Sudden—
Mist grow thick—
Mist-of-Great-No-Thing—drift through Blue-Flowers—

not see Blue-Flowers—
not see Wolf-Woman—
not see She -Wolf—

Raven Fly on— through Mist—

In this book, Barbara Grenfell Fairhead has successfully captured quicksilver – the inchoate, the unintelligible, the mystery of the landscape of the primordial mind. It is an extraordinary achievement. The only other book that came to mind while reading it is the award-winning book, *Riddley Walker* by Russell Hoban. Her book takes us even deeper into the early landscape of language and the earliest human earth.

Julian Roup
(journalist and author of *Life in a Time of Plague*)

This remarkable tale is a powerful reimagining of our species' unfolding and its future potential. Rio Abajo Rio is many things at once – part post-creation myth, part evocation of the first words ever spoken, it is simultaneously a projection of a post-apocalyptic society. This brave book is not easily described because Barbara Fairhead's narrative defies linearity in time and telling. The narration transports readers to a time and place when language was in formation and identity was fluid. Characters morph and shift with their emerging consciousness.

Liesl Jobson
(award winning writer, arts journalist and musician)

Barbara Grenfell Fairhead was born in the United Kingdom in 1939 and has lived most of her life in South Africa. After her first visit to New Mexico in the early 1990s it became her second home. She made many extended visits over a period of twenty years, staying in her casita close to Black Mesa. She is an artist, writer, poet and lyricist, and lives in Cape Town with her husband, singer-songwriter, poet and editor Jacques Coetzee. Her previous novels, *Of Death and Beauty* and *Whereof One Cannot Speak*, were also published by Sunstone Press.

ISBN 978-1-928433-32-3

90000

9 781928 433323

Printed in the United States
by Baker & Taylor Publisher Services